CREATURES OF LEGEND

WEREWOLVES

by Allan Morey

Content Consultant
Michael Delahoyde, PhD
Washington State University

CORE
LIBRARY

Published by ABDO Publishing Company, PO Box 398166, Minneapolis, MN 55439. Copyright © 2014 by Abdo Consulting Group, Inc. International copyrights reserved in all countries. No part of this book may be reproduced in any form without written permission from the publisher. The Core Library™ is a trademark and logo of ABDO Publishing Company.

Printed in the United States of America,
North Mankato, Minnesota
092013
012014

Editor: Lauren Coss
Series Designer: Becky Daum

Library of Congress Cataloging-in-Publication Data
Morey, Allan.
  Werewolves / by Allan Morey.
     pages cm. -- (Creatures of legend)
  Includes index.
  ISBN 978-1-62403-155-7
1. Werewolves--Juvenile literature. I. Title.
  GR830.W4M67 2014
  398.24'54--dc23
                              2013031417

Photo Credits: Shutterstock Images, cover, 1, 7; Lukiyanova Natalia/ Shutterstock Images, 4; Thinkstock, 8, 30, 45; Barbara Walton/epa/Corbis, 10; Chronicle/Alamy, 12; Ivy Close Images/Alamy, 15; Lordprice Collection/ Alamy, 16; Ivy Close Images/Alamy, 18; Mary Evans Picture Library/Alamy, 20; Oronoz/SuperStock, 22, 42; Patrick Aventurier/Gamma-Rapho/Getty Images, 27; Red Line Editorial, 29, 43 (top); MGM/Everett Collection, 32; Everett Collection, 34; Universal/Everett Collection, 37; Warner Brothers/ Everett Collection, 39; AF archive/Alamy, 40, 43 (bottom)

CONTENTS

CHAPTER ONE

ON A FULL MOON

It's a cold and foggy night. Dylan is heading home from his friend's house. It's late. Later than he had planned to be out. He had lost track of the time while reading his friend's new comic books. He knows his parents must be worried.

Dylan cuts through the neighborhood park. He half walks, half runs along the paved trail. He has taken this shortcut many times before. But tonight

Legends surrounding werewolves have been a part of cultures around the world for thousands of years.

the woods feel eerie. The moon is full. Dark shadows dance between the trees. An owl hoots in the distance.

Dylan pauses at a bend in the path to look up at the big silver moon. It peeks over the trees and lights up the path beneath his feet. He is thankful for the moonlight illuminating his way.

"Aaarrroooo!"

A howl echoes through the night and sends shivers down Dylan's spine. He picks up his pace to a quick jog.

Moments later, he hears another howl.

"AAARRROOOO!"

This time the howl is louder.

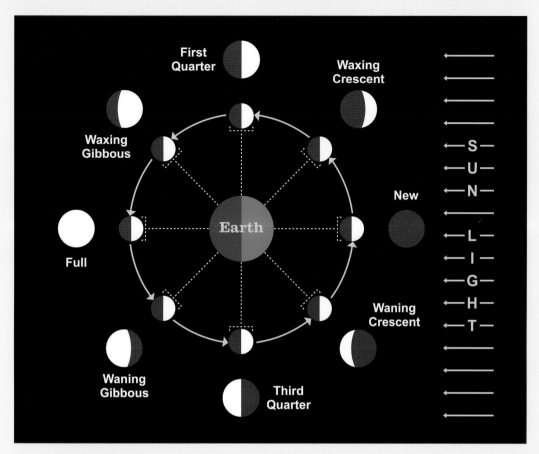

Lunar Cycle

Some cultures believe evil creatures, such as werewolves, are strongest during a full moon. As the moon and Earth circle the sun, sunlight shines on different parts of the moon and causes the phases of the lunar cycle. A full moon appears approximately every 29 days. Find out what time the moon will be visible where you live. Then compare the moon you see with the diagram above. Based on this diagram, how long will it be until the next full moon?

Fear moves Dylan forward. He ignores the branches slapping at his arms and his face as he sprints down the narrow path.

In many modern legends, werewolves can only transform during the full moon.

Dylan feels eyes on him. A dark shadow is flitting between the trees. Then he hears a creepy growl. He is almost home.

Dylan bursts from the woods as the path ends and meets up with the sidewalk that will take him home. He turns to run toward his house. Just then, a large hairy form leaps from the trees. It tackles him. Dylan feels a sharp pain on his cheek as he is slammed to the ground.

"Hey! Leave him alone!" a familiar voice yells from down the street. It's Dylan's father running toward him. The creature looks from Dylan's dad to Dylan and back to his dad again. Then it darts off into the trees.

"You okay?" his dad asks, helping Dylan to his feet.

"Yeah, I think so," he says, brushing the dirt off his jeans.

"I'm glad I came out to meet you," his dad says. "I was getting worried."

Dylan is shaken up. But now that his dad is with him he feels safe.

"Do you know who attacked you?" his dad asks.

"Who?" Dylan says, confused. "Don't you mean what? I thought it was a wolf."

Mistaken Identity

Dylan's story is fictional. However, some real people have been mistakenly called werewolves. Some of them suffered from hypertrichosis, sometimes called the "werewolf syndrome." This is a rare disease involving excessive hair growth. People once believed that having unusual growth of hair was a trait of a werewolf. During the 1800s and 1900s, people suffering from hypertrichosis often performed in circus sideshows.

Supatra Sasuphan, *left*, has a disease that causes her to grow more hair than most other humans.

"Are you sure?" his dad asks. "He ran off on two legs."

Dylan's mom is waiting for them in the kitchen as they walk into the house. "What's that?" she asks, as she wipes away a blood smear on Dylan's cheek.

Dylan tells her about his attack. "I got scratched when I fell," he says. *Or bit*, he thinks.

"Well, it's nothing," Dylan's mom says. "There's not even a mark."

"That's weird," Dylan says, rubbing his cheek. He remembers the sharp pain he felt when he was

EXPLORE ONLINE

Chapter One discusses people with a disease that causes them to grow an unusual amount of hair. The Web site below introduces Supatra Sasuphan, a girl from Thailand who set the Guinness World Record for "Hairiest Teenager" in 2010. As you know, every source is different. How is the information on this Web site different from the information on hypertrichosis in this chapter? How is it the same? How does reading about Supatra's experience help you understand hypertrichosis?

Supatra Sasuphan
www.mycorelibrary.com/werewolves

attacked. What Dylan doesn't realize is that he has had an encounter with a werewolf. Legends of these savage creatures have existed for thousands of years. In modern stories, anyone who survives a werewolf bite will turn into one at the next full moon. Could Dylan become a werewolf himself?

AAARRROOOO!

CHAPTER TWO

HOWLING AT THE MOON

The word *werewolf* comes from the Old English words *wer*, for "man," and *wulf*, meaning "wolf." According to legend, werewolves are shape-shifters. They are humans who can turn into wolves or wolf-like creatures. In some myths, werewolves are able to transform at will. Other legends require an outside force, such as the full moon.

In most older werewolf legends, humans fully transform into wolves.

Werecats?

In countries without many wolves, people were said to change into other animals. Usually people were suspected of changing into the animals people feared the most, often large cats. In Asia weretigers were said to prowl the night. Africa had legends of wereleopards and werelions. South American mythology told of werejaguars.

In most ancient legends, humans completely transform into wolves. In modern legends, werewolves often look somewhat human, even in their wolf forms. Werewolves have excellent senses. They are usually stronger and faster than regular humans or wolves. In many legends, werewolves have no control over their actions while in wolf form. In some modern versions of the werewolf legend, only a silver bullet can kill the beast.

Fighting Fiercely

Believe it or not, becoming a werewolf wasn't always seen as a curse. In some ancient stories, people used potions or spells to transform themselves into

While in wolf form, a werewolf is said to attack and eat humans and animals.

wolves. Others believed they could become wolves by wearing wolf skin. In the 1500s, Swedish writer Olaus Magnus wrote *History of the Northern Peoples*. His book included an account of people wearing wolf skin pelts and uttering magic words to turn themselves into wolves.

In the *Völsunga Saga*, an ancient Scandinavian tale from the 1200s, warriors wore wolf skins. They

15

In many legends, a werewolf's bite turns its victim into a werewolf.

believed fighting with a wolf's fierceness would help them win battles.

Becoming a Werewolf

How does a person become a werewolf? That depends on when you lived. Long ago, people believed someone who drank water from a wolf's footprint would become a werewolf. Other legends state children born during a full moon became werewolves. In France and Germany, it was once thought that people who fell asleep with the full moon shining on their faces could turn into werewolves.

The most common belief is that anyone who survives being bitten by a werewolf will eventually change into one. No one is really sure how this idea entered werewolf mythology. Some historians believe this idea is based on the rabies disease. Animals infected with rabies can pass the disease to humans by biting them.

Rabies

Rabies is a disease in mammals that can be transmitted through the bite of an infected animal. It affects the nervous system and causes animals to act in unpredictable ways. Nocturnal animals may roam around in the day. Friendly pets might become overly aggressive. Raccoons, skunks, and bats are common carriers of rabies. People can get this disease if bitten by an animal carrying it. Infected people might act confused and nervous. They might salivate more, as a hungry dog would. At one time, people suffering from rabies were thought to be werewolves.

Most werewolves keep some of their wolf-like characteristics when in their human forms.

Spotting a Werewolf

Many legends include telltale signs that a person is a werewolf. In older legends, werewolves were said to have middle and ring fingers that were the same length. Suspected werewolves were often extra hairy in their human forms. They were also unusually aggressive. As humans, werewolves grew long or curved, sharp fingernails. However, in most modern legends, the beast of a werewolf often only fully comes out when the moon is full.

Many early beliefs about werewolves involved witchcraft. Witches and warlocks were said to have the power to change into animal form by using potions or spells. The *zagovór*, or "spell," below is from the book *The Songs of the Russian People*, written by W. R. S. Ralston in 1872:

In the ocean sea, on the island Buyan, in the open plain, shines the moon upon an aspen stump, into the green wood, into the spreading vale. Around the stump goes a shaggy wolf; under his teeth are all the horned cattle; but into the wood the wolf goes not, in the vale the wolf does not roam. Moon, moon! Golden horns! Melt the bullet, blunt the knife, rot the cudgel, strike fear into man, beast, and reptile, so that they may not seize the gray wolf, nor tear from him his warm hide. My word is firm, firmer than sleep or the strength of heroes.

Source: W. R. S. Ralston. The Songs of the Russian People. London, UK: Ellis and Green, 1872. Print. 406.

Consider Your Audience

Read this passage carefully. Ask an adult to help you look up any words you don't know. How would you change this spell to include ideas about today's werewolves? Are there any items you might need to make the spell work?

CHAPTER THREE

THE FIRST WEREWOLVES

Historians may never know who first scared whom with terrifying tales of werewolves. But some people believe the first werewolf was Enkidu. Enkidu is a character from the *Epic of Gilgamesh*, a story dating back to 2000 BCE. Enkidu is a hairy beast man. According to the story, he was created from mud and the spit of a goddess. This goddess was angry with Gilgamesh, the ruler of the

People's fears of wolves likely led to some of the first werewolf legends.

Lycaon was punished by being turned into a wolf.

ancient civilization of Sumer. She sends Enkidu to kill him. But Gilgamesh wins their battle. Instead of killing the beast man, the king befriends Enkidu. The pair end up having several adventures together.

Ancient Werewolves

King Lycaon was probably the first person rumored to change into a wolf and take on wolf-like characteristics. He was a legendary Greek ruler from thousands of years ago. Roman poet Ovid retells the story of Lycaon in his long poem *Metamorphoses*, written in 8 CE. According to Ovid, Lycaon is a brutal king. He wants to test Zeus, ruler of the gods, to prove he is divine. Lycaon kills a servant and secretly feeds him to Zeus. The god is furious at the king. As punishment, Zeus turns Lycaon into a wolf. But the king's cruel ways stay with him in wolf form. He becomes a fearsome beast that terrorizes nearby villages.

In about the 400s BCE, Greek historian Herodotus may have been the first to record the possible existence of real werewolves. Herodotus spent much of his life traveling the ancient world. He published a text titled *History*. In the book, Herodotus describes the people he met during his travels throughout the ancient world. He mentions the Neuri, who lived in Eastern Europe.

The Neuri were said to be conjurers, people who performed magic. Once a year, Herodotus wrote, the Neuri turn themselves into wolves. After a few days, they change back into humans. Some historians think the Neuri dressed in wolf skins for hunting. Similar to the Scandinavian hunters described in *Völsunga Saga*, the Neuri may have believed the skins gave them special hunting abilities. Herodotus simply mistook a hunter dressed in wolf skins as a werewolf.

The Father of History

Herodotus wrote some of the earliest known history books. He was probably the first historian to travel throughout the ancient world. Herodotus included stories he learned from his many travels, such as those of the Neuri, in *History*. He did firsthand research on the places and people he wrote about. Herodotus asked the people he met about their customs and beliefs.

Witchcraft and Wolves

Herodotus's story was a sign of changing beliefs in the world. As Christianity spread throughout Europe, stories about werewolves changed. Instead of gods turning people into wolves, witchcraft was to blame. Witches were said to have evil powers. They could change themselves into animals at will. They could also turn others into animals. Many people believed the wild tales about witchcraft being used to transform people into wolves. Some people believed they were werewolves themselves.

Lycanthropy

Many people who believed they were werewolves were actually suffering from a mental illness. People with lycanthropy think they are wolves. They may howl or take on other wolf-like traits. Hundreds of years ago, most people did not recognize lycanthropy as a mental illness. They believed people with the condition were actually werewolves.

It was dangerous for a person to be considered a werewolf. From ancient times to the 1700s, wolves were the top predator in Europe. Europeans feared the creatures. Wolves were believed to be aggressive and dangerous. They often killed livestock. Hungry wolves were even known to attack people. Rulers often hired hunters to kill wolves. People accused of

Beast of Gévaudan

In the 1760s a mysterious beast terrorized the region of Gévaudan, France. The creature was said to look similar to a large wolf. However unlike most wolves, it seemed to prefer eating humans to livestock. Many people believed it was a werewolf. The king of France organized hunts to capture the beast. But hunters couldn't manage to kill the animal. The attacks continued. The beast is believed to have killed or injured hundreds before it was finally killed. Historians still don't know what type of creature the Beast of Gévaudan really was.

being werewolves were usually killed as well.

Loup-Garous

Some of the most frequent werewolf reports came from France. In the 1500s, thousands of people were accused of being *loup-garous*, which is French for "werewolves." Many of these people were executed. In the late 1500s, near the French village of Dole, a dead child was found. Rumors said teeth marks covered his arms and legs. These were telltale signs of a werewolf attack.

The Beast of Gévaudan was a real werewolf-like creature that terrorized France in the 1700s.

Days later a group of villagers heard a girl scream. Then they heard a howl. As the villagers rushed to help the girl, a creature ran off on all fours. Some thought it looked like Gilles Gamier, a hermit living on the edge of town. When captured, Gamier insisted he had turned into a wolf to commit his crimes. But no one ever saw him change. He was eventually executed.

By the 1800s, wolves were becoming much less common in western Europe. Rulers continued hiring hunters to kill wolves through the early 1900s. By this time wolves were extinct from much of Europe, including England and France. Gradually the European werewolf faded into legend.

North American Legends

Werewolf myths didn't exist only in European cultures. Many Native-American tribes had werewolf legends of their own. However, Native Americans viewed wolves very differently from Europeans. Many Native Americans admired wolves instead of fearing them. In North America, wolves were seen as mighty hunters. They lived in strong family units and defended their pack mates. These were considered honorable traits. To be compared to a wolf was high praise, not a curse. In some tribes, such as the Pawnee, warriors dressed in wolf skins. They hoped the skins would give them wolf-like powers in battle or while hunting.

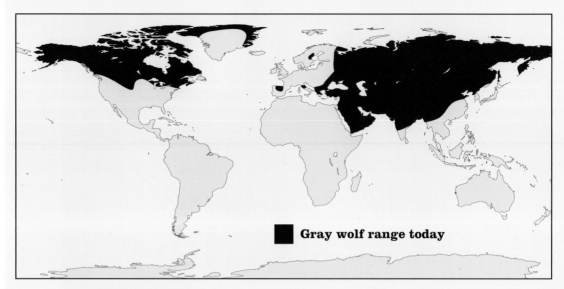

Gray wolf range today

Wolf Extinction

Gray wolves once roamed throughout western Europe, North America, and North Africa. Today they are only found in the shaded areas on the map above. How do you think the wolves' loss of range affected the werewolf legend? How might the legend change again if wolves start moving back into their former territory?

However, not all Native-American werewolf legends were positive. Navajo legends of the southwestern United States tell of evil shape-shifters known as skinwalkers. Skinwalkers look like normal people in daylight. But at night, they have the ability to change into any animal, often an owl, coyote, or wolf. According to some legends, skinwalkers use an animal pelt to make this transformation. In some

Many Native-American tribes hold a deep respect for wolves.

versions of the legend, skinwalkers can even take on the appearance of another person.

Today, few people still believe in werewolves. However, the world's fascination with them remains strong.

In *Metamorphoses*, Roman poet Ovid uses popular myths to tell the history of the world. In one myth, Ovid describes King Lycaon as a wolf:

> [Lycaon] himself ran in terror, and reaching the silent fields howled aloud, frustrated of speech. Foaming at the mouth, and greedy as ever for killing, he turned against the sheep, still delighting in blood. His clothes became bristling hair, his arms became legs. He was a wolf, but kept some vestige of his former shape. There were the same gray hairs, the same violent face, the same glittering eyes, the same savage image.

Source: Ovid. Metamorphoses *Book 1:199–243. Trans. Anthony S. Kline.* The Ovid Collection. *University of Virginia Library, 2000. Web. Accessed August 13, 2013.*

What's the Big Idea?

In ancient times, people sometimes used myths to explain why things happened in the world. Some myths explain how the world was created. Others explain why the sun rises. Since people cannot really turn into wolves, what do you think this myth is saying about King Lycaon?

CHAPTER FOUR

MODERN WEREWOLVES

Early myths and legends about werewolves differ in many ways from how we view these fictional beasts today. For one, most older werewolf myths involve people who completely transformed into wolves. In many modern legends, werewolves walk on two legs.

In the 1985 film *Teen Wolf*, actor Michael J. Fox plays an ordinary high school student who learns he is a werewolf.

Werewolf of London popularized the idea of a werewolf that walks on two legs.

Two Legs and Silver

The two-legged werewolf was first shown on screen in the 1935 film *Werewolf of London*. In the film a werewolf bites English botanist Wilfred Glendon. Then the full moon causes Glendon to turn into a half-man, half-wolf creature that roams London's streets. A police officer eventually manages to shoot and kill Glendon. Many later movies would also feature werewolves with similar, human-like appearances.

Another feature of modern werewolf mythology was introduced in 1936. In most early legends, regular weapons can kill a werewolf. But in many modern legends, werewolves must be killed with a silver weapon. French author Abel Chevalley introduced this idea in his 1936 novel retelling the story of the Beast of Gévaudan. This mysterious wolf-like creature terrorized France in the

The Magic of Silver

In ancient times silver was connected to the gods of the moon. For example, Artemis, the Greek goddess of the hunt and the moon, was often armed with a silver bow. Silver has long been thought to have healing abilities. In ancient times, some people stored water in silver urns to prevent it from going bad. Silver is believed to prevent the growth of germs, viruses, and bacteria. Silver nitrate is still used today to fight infections.

1700s. In the novel, a silver bullet is required to kill the creature.

Werewolves on the Big Screen

In 1941 these modern ideas were combined in one of the most famous horror films of all time—*The Wolf Man*. In the movie a werewolf bites Larry Talbot, played by actor Lon Chaney Jr. Talbot changes into a half-man, half-wolf creature and attacks a local gravedigger. He stalks the town until his father finally kills him using a silver cane.

Audiences were frightened and amazed by Lon Chaney Jr.'s transformation into the Wolf Man. The film was so popular that the character appeared in several other movies, including 1943's *Frankenstein Meets the Wolf Man* and *House of Dracula* in 1945.

As special effects improved, werewolf films became even more impressive. In 1981 the film *An American Werewolf in London* made werewolf history. The film tells the story of David Kessler, an American tourist. He is traveling through England

Kessler's realistic and dramatic transformation into a werewolf amazed audiences.

when a werewolf bites him. At the full moon, he transforms into a werewolf. The movie suggests that the transformation into a werewolf is painful.

The audience hears the sounds of bones crunching as Kessler transforms. Through special effects viewers see Kessler's face lengthen into a wolf's snout. Hair sprouts on his back. His hands and feet grow into paws.

In 1985 actor Michael J. Fox played a different kind of werewolf in the film *Teen Wolf*. Fox's character, high school student Scott Howard, unexpectedly turns into a werewolf one day. He learns his father is also a werewolf. Instead of attacking people, Scott transforms during basketball games to help his team win.

We Like to Be Scared

In the 1800s many people were curious about creatures from myth and folklore. This fascination led to a popular genre of fiction called gothic horror. This genre features stories that combined romance and supernatural elements. Authors wrote about witches, vampires, ghosts, and of course, werewolves. One popular scary tale was *Wagner the Wehr-Wolf*, written in 1846 by George W. M. Reynolds. It tells of a man cursed to turn into a wolf every full moon. In the 1900s, the genre evolved into modern horror fiction.

In *The Prisoner of Azkaban*, Harry Potter's teacher Remus Lupin loses all memory of his human self when he transforms into a werewolf.

Werewolves Today

In recent years, werewolves have continued to pop up in popular books, television shows, and movies. In the Harry Potter books, written by J. K. Rowling from 1997 to 2007, one of Harry Potter's teachers, Remus Lupin, is a werewolf. The books were later made into a popular film series.

In the Twilight Saga, werewolf Jacob Black can transform whenever he chooses. He does not need a full moon.

In the television series *Teen Wolf*, loosely based on the 1985 film, a teenage boy struggles with life as a modern-day werewolf. The show first aired in 2011.

Werewolves also play an important role in the Twilight Saga, a young adult book series written by Stephenie Meyer between 2005 and 2008. The books were so popular they were made into movies.

In the Twilight Saga, the character Jacob Black is part of a Native-American tribe in Washington State. Some members of the tribe can transform into huge wolves. Jacob and the other members of his pack keep their human memories and emotions while in wolf form.

The werewolf legend has gone through many transformations since it first appeared in ancient times. Few people believe in werewolves today. But the myth remains as strong as ever.

EXPLORE ONLINE

Robert Louis Stevenson published his novel *The Strange Case of Dr. Jekyll and Mr. Hyde* in 1886. While reading the summary of his story at the link below, do you see any similarities to the werewolf stories discussed in Chapters Two, Three, and Four? Do you think Mr. Hyde might be considered a werewolf? Are there other figures in popular culture that transform like werewolves?

The Strange Case of Dr. Jekyll and Mr. Hyde
www.mycorelibrary.com/werewolves

Enkidu

Uruk, Sumer

In a tale more than 4,000 years old, the Sumerian goddess Aruru creates Enkidu, a wolf-like beast man, from mud and spit. He befriends Gilgamesh, the Sumerian ruler.

King Lycaon

Arcadia, Greece

In *Metamorphoses*, written in approximately 8 CE, Roman poet Ovid describes King Lycaon. According to Ovid, the mythical Greek god Zeus turns King Lycaon into a wolf as punishment. This myth is the first known story in which a man is turned into a wolf.

The Neuri

Eastern Europe

In *History*, written in approximately 450 BCE, Herodotus gives an account of the Neuri, who are said to change into wolves once a year.

The Beast of Gévaudan

Gévaudan, France

According to historical records, more than 100 people were killed in south-central France by a wolf-like creature nicknamed the Beast of Gévaudan. Historians aren't sure what type of animal the beast really was.

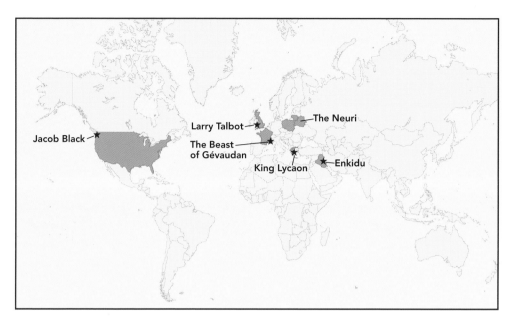

Larry Talbot

Wales, United Kingdom

The movie *The Wolf Man*, released in 1941, helped make the werewolf one of the most popular movie monsters. After being bitten by a werewolf, Talbot, played by Lon Chaney Jr., transforms into a werewolf. Chaney's character was so popular that it appeared in several other movies made in the 1940s.

Jacob Black

Forks, Washington

Jacob Black is a character from author Stephenie Meyer's popular young adult series the Twilight Saga, written between 2005 and 2008. Jacob is a member of a tribe of Native Americans who can change into wolves. The books were later made into popular films.

You Are There

Chapter Three of this book discusses the Beast of Gévaudan. Imagine you are a hunter hired to kill the beast. Where do you look for it? What would you use to hunt a werewolf? What would you bring to protect yourself?

Take a Stand

Imagine you are at a trial in the 1500s for someone who has been accused of being a werewolf. You believe the person is innocent. What modern information could you use to help defend the accused werewolf? Using the information you learned in this book, write a paragraph persuading the jury that the accused person is not actually a werewolf. Be sure to include facts and details to support your ideas.

Surprise Me

Chapter Two discussed some of the legends surrounding how a person might become a werewolf. When read about today, some of these beliefs can be surprising. What did you think was the most surprising belief about how someone might become a werewolf? What surprised you most about it?

Say What?

Learning about werewolves can mean learning a lot of new vocabulary. Find five words in this book that are new to you. Use a dictionary to look up their meanings, and use each word in a sentence. Then write the meanings in your own words.

GLOSSARY

aggressive
violent or threatening

botanist
a scientist who specializes in studying plants

conjurer
a person who performs magic

epic
a long story or poem, usually with historical subject matter

genre
a certain category of book, movie, or other creative work

hermit
a person who lives alone and prefers to stay away from people

lycanthropy
a condition in which people believe they are wolves

nocturnal
most active at night

pelt
animal skin

savage
especially fierce or cruel

supernatural
outside the normal realm of human existence, such as spirits, vampires, and werewolves

transform
to change

LEARN MORE

Books

Hamilton, S. L. *Werewolves*. Edina, MN: ABDO, 2010.

Hirschmann, Kris. *The Werewolf*. San Diego, CA: ReferencePoint Press, 2012.

Lestrade, Ursula. *The Werewolf Hunter's Guide*. Mankato, MN: Sea-to-Sea, 2012.

Web Links

To learn more about werewolves, visit ABDO Publishing Company online at **www.abdopublishing.com**. Web sites about werewolves are featured on our Book Links page. These links are routinely monitored and updated to provide the most current information available. Visit **www.mycorelibrary.com** for free additional tools for teachers and students.

INDEX

ABOUT THE AUTHOR

Allan Morey grew up on a farm in central Wisconsin, where he had a pet pig named Pete. Allan's early love of animals has stayed with him his entire life. He's had pet fish, mice, gerbils, cockatiels, cats, and even a ferret.